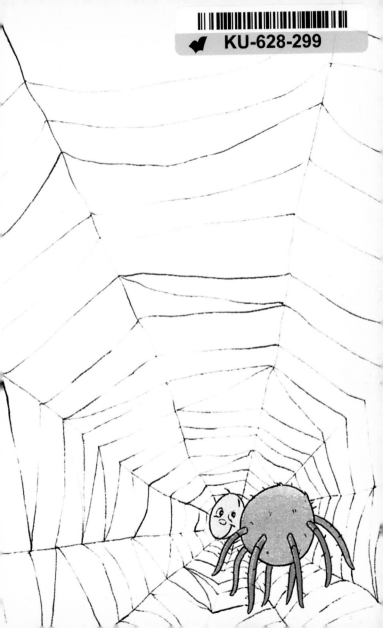

© 1994 Geddes & Grosset Ltd
Published by Geddes & Grosset Ltd,
New Lanark, Scotland.

ISBN 1 85534 578 1

Printed and bound in Slovenia.

Snow White and the Seven Dwarfs

Retold by Judy Hamilton
Illustrated by Lindsay Duff

Tarantula Books

In a grand castle far way there once lived a young girl called Snow White with her father the king and stepmother the queen. Snow White was beautiful, with hair as black as ebony, lips red as roses and skin as white as the snow. Everyone loved Snow White except her stepmother, who was jealous of her beauty. She gave Snow White the hardest chores to do and treated her unkindly. But Snow White remained cheerful.

Her stepmother had a magic mirror in her bedroom. Every day she would ask it:

"Mirror, mirror on the wall.

Who is the fairest of them all?"

And every day the mirror would answer:

"You, my queen, are the fairest of them all."

But Snow White grew more beautiful every day and one day, when the queen went to her mirror, she did not get the answer that she expected. As usual, the queen asked:

"Mirror, mirror on the wall
Who is the fairest of them all?"

In answer, the mirror said:

"Alas my Queen, there is one fairer than thee,
Snow white skin, rose red lips and hair of ebony."

The queen knew that the mirror meant Snow White. Furious, she summoned her head huntsman. She wanted rid of Snow White for ever.

"Take the girl to the forest," she screamed, "and kill her! Bring me back her heart!"

Reluctantly, the huntsman went to do her bidding.

The huntsman walked slowly into the forest with Snow White. He was too scared of the queen to disobey her, but he loved Snow White and could never kill her. He turned to Snow White.

"Run for your life, Snow White, and don't come back. The queen must never see you again!" Snow White ran off. Then the huntsman shot a deer with his crossbow and took its heart back to the queen instead of Snow White's heart.

Snow White ran until she was out of breath. The huntsman had saved her life, but she had nowhere to go. The forest was frightening in the dark, and full of strange noises. What would she do?

She wandered on until evening, when she came to a clearing. There she saw a small cottage.

Snow White knocked on the door, but there was no answer. She opened the door and went in. She saw a table with seven little chairs round it. By the fireplace were seven tiny pairs of slippers. On the door were seven coathooks. But everywhere Snow White looked there was dirt and dust. She set about clearing up and soon had everything spick and span. Then she went upstairs and found seven little beds and seven nightgowns crumpled on the floor. She tidied up, and sat down on one bed to rest.

"What a strange little house!" she thought. Then, worn out, she fell asleep.

When Snow White awoke, seven little faces stared at her from the foot of the bed.

"Who are you?" asked one of the little men.

"I am Snow White," said Snow White. "I am sorry to have come in uninvited. Who are you?"

"We are the seven dwarfs," another little man spoke up. "Don't worry about coming in here. You tidied up so beautifully! But why are you here?"

So Snow White told the seven dwarfs all about her stepmother and explained that she had nowhere to go. The dwarfs muttered amongst themselves for a moment, then spoke together.

"You may stay here with us if you like. We can build a bed for you to sleep in downstairs."

"Thank you," said Snow White, "but I must repay you. Let me be your housekeeper!"

And so Snow White settled in with the dwarfs. Every day the seven dwarfs set off to the mine where they worked, and every evening they returned to eat with Snow White. Snow White loved the seven little men; they were funny and friendly. The dwarfs adored Snow White. The household was filled with laughter. Sometimes the dwarfs would tease Snow White,

"One day you will be carried off by a prince!"

Snow White would laugh, saying,

"I have seven princes already!"

Sometimes she wondered if she would ever fall in love, but she was still happy.

But Snow White would not have felt so safe if she had known what her stepmother was up to.

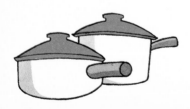

The queen was delighted to see the huntsman return with the deer's heart. Thinking that Snow White was dead, she did not consult her magic mirror for several days. But she still needed to be told how beautiful she was, so one day she went to the mirror again:

"Mirror, mirror on the wall,
Who is the fairest of them all?"

The mirror's reply filled her with rage:

"Alas, Queen, Snow White is alive and well,
Deep in the forest, safe she dwells,
She is the fairest of them all."

At once the queen sent men to find Snow White.

"When you find her, tell me!" she commanded. "I will deal with Snow White myself!"

The queen's men searched for Snow White in the forest for days. The queen grew angrier and angrier. Then finally, early one morning, one of the men found the cottage of the seven dwarfs. He watched until he saw Snow White coming out of the tiny door to go and collect firewood. He ran all the way back to the castle to tell the queen what he had seen.

"She lives with seven dwarfs, your majesty," he told her, "but she is alone in the cottage all day when they go to work in the mines."

The queen cackled as she prepared to carry out her evil plan. She worked all night and when she left the castle early the next morning, nobody recognized her as the queen.

Snow White was preparing the supper when a knock came on the door of the tiny cottage. When she opened the door, she saw a wizened old woman dressed in rags, carrying a basket of apples.

"Buy my apples, dear," said the woman.

Snow White looked at the apples; shiny and red without a bruise or a blemish.

"Try one, my dear, I'm sure you will like it!" The old woman held out one of the apples to Snow White. Snow White took one and raised it to her lips. The old woman watched eagerly. No sooner had Snow White taken the first bite, when she fell to the ground in a dreamless sleep.

"She's gone!" cackled the old woman.

It was the queen!

The seven dwarfs were coming back from work, when they caught sight of a strange woman running from the cottage. She was dressed as an old woman and looked like an old woman, but she ran with the strength and speed of someone much younger. The dwarfs became suspicious.

"Snow White is in danger!"

The voice of the queen cackled in reply,

"Snow White is DEAD!"

The dwarfs gave chase. They knew the forest better than the queen, and could move faster. They spread out to surround her, so that she had only one path left open; it led up a steep cliff-face. Half-way up, the rocks crumbled beneath her feet, and she fell.

The queen was dead, but the dwarfs wanted to save Snow White. Leaving the queen where she lay, they hurried back to the cottage. Snow White lay in the doorway, her skin paler than ever. She did not seem to be breathing.

The dwarfs' hearts were heavy as they carried Snow White into the cottage and laid her on her bed. Then one of them noticed that Snow White was breathing, very faintly. The apple had poisoned her, but had not killed her. The dwarfs made a special bed for Snow White, but many weeks passed and still she did not wake up.

Then one day a prince from a nearby kingdom was riding in the forest and stopped at the cottage to ask for a drink of water.

The dwarfs took the prince to see Snow White and told him what had happened. The prince thought she looked beautiful, surrounded by flowers which the dwarfs had picked, and felt sad that no one could wake her. He leant over and gently kissed her lips. The kiss from the prince worked great magic, for at that very moment Snow White opened her eyes. The dwarfs jumped for joy to see Snow White well again.

The prince and Snow White fell in love. It was just as the dwarfs had said long ago; a handsome prince was to carry her off.

But Snow White did not leave the dwarfs. A special house was built beside the prince's palace, to keep them close to her always.